To:

From:

D0810729

A CENTURY OF

Christmas Memories

1900-1999

By the Editors of Peter Pauper Press

PETER PAUPER PRESS, INC.
White Plains, New York

PETER PAUPER PRESS
Fine Books and Gifts Since 1928

Our Company

In 1928, at the age of twenty-two, Peter Beilenson began printing books on a small press in the basement of his parents' home in Larchmont, New York. Peter—and later his wife, Edna—sought to create fine books that sold at "prices even a pauper could afford."

Today, still family owned and operated, Peter Pauper Press continues to honor our founders' legacy—and our customers' expectations—of beauty, quality, and value.

Designed by Heather Zschock

Picture credits appear on page 120

Copyright © 2009
Peter Pauper Press, Inc.
202 Mamaroneck Avenue
White Plains, NY 10601
All rights reserved
ISBN 978-1-59359-769-6
Printed in China
7 6 5

A CENTURY OF

Christmas Memories

1900 - 1999

Contents

Introduction

Laura Ingalls Wilder once said, "We are better throughout the year for having, in spirit, become a child again at Christmas-time." Let this merry little keepsake book whisk you back in time to childhood and beyond to celebrate the wonders of Christmases past! *A Century of Christmas Memories* commemorates 100 years of seasonal firsts and favorites—movies, songs, events, traditions, toys, and games—year by year, decade by decade, from 1900 through the 1990s. Enjoy fond memories of surprises under the tree, from Pogo Sticks, Tinker Toys, and Tiddlywinks to Hula Hoops, Etch-A-Sketch, Barney, and the Smurfs. Revisit moving holiday moments, from the first tree at Rockefeller

Center to Bob Hope's first USO show, and from watching *It's a Wonderful Life* or *A Christmas Story* to getting into the holiday swing with *Santa Claus Blues* or *Grandma Got Run Over by a Reindeer*. You'll bask in the warm fuzzies of these fun and festive yuletide trimmings, illustrated with nostalgic photographs throughout. Season's readings!

Remembering the **1900s**

As the century began, Americans embraced the values and traditions of
Christmas with ever more public celebrations. The world was changing fast, but
the holiday offered the unity of brotherhood, good will, and peace. The average
worker made $13 for a 59-hour work week. Only 8,000 cars puttered along
the nation's ten miles of paved road, and Teddy Roosevelt was president for most
of the decade. One of the most popular gifts was his namesake, the teddy bear.
Many other soon-to-be staples of the season—including electric Christmas lights,
radio, and film—were in their infancy.

1900

At the turn of the century, one in five American families enjoy
a Christmas tree in their homes. These lucky New York City
public school students got to have one in their classroom! But
electrically lit Christmas trees are still a novelty reserved for
the privileged. A typical lighted tree costs about $300 (roughly
$2,000 in today's money). The price includes a wireman's serv-
ices and a generator.

- On Christmas Day in 1900, ornithologist Frank Chapman proposes *counting* birds rather than *hunting* birds with his introduction of the **Christmas Bird Count.** This bird conservation tradition persists within the Audubon Society to this day.

- *The Wonderful Wizard of Oz* by L. Frank Baum is published in September, in time to become a cherished Christmas present.

- Hershey introduces the original **Hershey's milk chocolate bar**—a tasty stocking stuffer!

- Popular **Christmas toys of 1900** include sleds (selling for 98 cents each), sleeping eyes dolls (89 cents each), doll cradles (10 cents each), and ice skates (49 cents per pair).

1901

- The first **Christmas tree farm** is started just outside Trenton, New Jersey, when W. V. McGalliard plants 25,000 Norway spruce trees.

- On December 10, 1901, the **first Nobel Prizes** are awarded in the fields of physics, chemistry, medicine, literature, and peace. Alfred Nobel set up the award program to recognize people who have "conferred the greatest benefit on mankind"—a *noble* initiative in keeping with the holiday spirit!

- Conservationist President Theodore Roosevelt, concerned about the destruction of forests, decides not to have a **Christmas tree for the White House.** Today, people debate the consequences of using real vs. artificial trees, with many believing that if harvested correctly, real trees can be more environmentally sound than their artificial, and often petroleum-based, non-biodegradable counterparts.

With Joshua Lionel Cowen's invention of the **first electric train** for a store display window, trains are on track to become one of the century's most favored Christmas toys. Pictured here are cog-wheel trains and other toys, circa 1900.

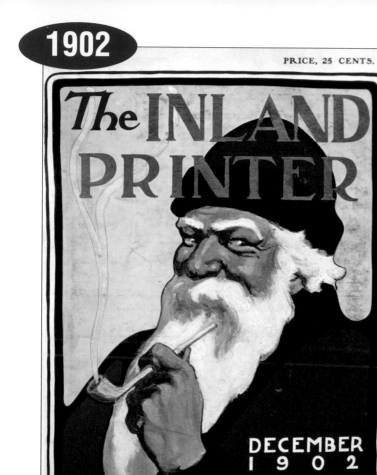

1902

PRICE, 25 CENTS.

The INLAND PRINTER

DECEMBER
1902

Father Christmas graces the cover of *The Inland Printer*. **Christmas-themed magazine covers** may seem commonplace today, but the practice of having a new cover for each issue of a periodical was first introduced by this influential magazine at the turn of the century.

- National Biscuit Company repackages its **animal crackers** in a red circus wagon box with a string attached—perfect for use as a Christmas tree ornament! The five-cent boxes were a hit and continue to be favorites today.

- The **teddy bear**, one of the world's most beloved Christmas toys, is born. Its origin is based on a story about President Theodore Roosevelt. In November 1902, "T. R." went on a bear-hunting trip, but he was unable to bag one himself. His hunting party hosts trapped a bear and tied it to a tree to offer the president an easy target. But Roosevelt refused, saying, "Spare the bear! I will not shoot a tethered animal." The incident becomes famous, and inspires Brooklyn shopkeepers Morris and Rose Michtom to make a cuddly stuffed bear toy and place it in their shop right at the height of the Christmas season. They name it "Teddy's bear."

1903

Huntley and Palmers Christmas cakes and biscuits are a holiday staple. Several festive delectables are shown here on their catalog!

- **Advent calendars** are introduced; they are attributed to printer Gerhard Lang. Legend has it Lang's mother gave her son a piece of cake or biscuit on each day in December, giving him something to look forward to as he counted down to Christmas. This inspired his creation of the calendars that offer children treats or favors for each day leading up to December 25.

Binney and Smith sells its first sets of **Crayola Crayons**. A box of eight sold for five cents, making a great stocking stuffer!

- General Electric begins mass production of **"festoons"—colorful strings of lights intended to decorate Christmas trees**. Though these are the first practical Christmas lights, they're still quite expensive—a set of 24 cost $12. And in 1903, the average weekly wage is $13.20.

Victor Herbert's operetta ***Babes in Toyland*** opens at the Majestic Theatre in New York and runs for 192 performances. The musical sets Mother Goose nursery rhyme characters in a Christmas theme.

The booming auto industry, reflected by this cover of the French magazine *La Vie au Grand Air*, is transforming the concept of **holiday travel**.

Christmas Seals are introduced by Danish postal clerk Einar Holboell. Intended as an extra charitable stamp for Christmas cards, the money aids children suffering from tuberculosis.

1905

Christmas Club savings accounts gain in popularity. The accounts enable people to sock away a little money each week. In December, the money is withdrawn for Christmas shopping. As seen in this 1905 photo, popular gifts include **soldier costumes**!

- The **town of Christmas, Arizona**, is founded; for years to come, people mail letters here just to get the collectible "Christmas" town postmark. Its post office closed in 1935, however, and Christmas is now officially listed as a ghost town.

- *The Spirit of Christmas*, a collection of Christmas stories by Henry Van Dyke, is published by Charles Scribner's Sons.

- *The Night Before Christmas*, a silent, nine-minute black-and-white film, entertains yuletide audiences.

1906

- The **first radio broadcast** takes place on Christmas Eve of this year. Canadian inventor Reginald Fessenden succeeds in transmitting voice and music to ships in the Atlantic Ocean. He plays a violin solo of "O Holy Night" and wishes everyone a Merry Christmas!

The **Christmas Snowstorm** takes the U.K. by surprise; the populace goes to bed under clear skies, but wakes up to a white Christmas! The storm deposits about four to twelve inches of snow overnight.

- O. Henry's **"The Gift of the Magi"** is published in the short story collection, *The Four Million*. The touching tale of unselfish love and gift-giving becomes a Christmas classic.

1907

- The African-American spiritual **"Go Tell It on the Mountain"** is published by John W. Work in *Folk Songs of the American Negro*. The song continues to be a favorite at Christmas concerts and church services throughout North America.

- Oklahoma becomes the last U.S. state to declare **Christmas a legal holiday**.

- In keeping with the Danish tradition begun in 1904 (see page 13), the U.S. introduces its own **Christmas Seals** and the American Lung Association is founded.

- The annual **Times Square New Year's Eve** ball drop begins. The first ball, made of iron and wood, weighs 700 pounds and gets its glitter from 100 25-watt light bulbs.

1908

A silent black-and-white movie adaptation of Charles Dickens's *A Christmas Carol* is released by Essanay Studios of Chicago on December 9.

- On Christmas Eve, the mayor of New York City issues a police order to **close down every movie theater** in Gotham, citing concern for public health as the cause. The city's small, cramped theaters are deemed unsafe dens of bacteria. Others believe the "moral" health of New York is the mayor's true concern. *Bah humbug, Scrooge!*

- John Scarpa starts the **first lighted boat parade** in Newport Beach, California. Boat owners still "deck the hulls" of their vessels with lights and decorations each year to celebrate the season.

The **Model T Ford** debuts in September, 1908, and is priced at an affordable $825. Even Santa can get new wheels!

The Avalanche

Vol. IX   Lubbock, Lubbock County, Texas, Friday, December 18, 1908.   No. 9

1909

Christmas postcards, a precursor to today's Christmas card, are a popular way to send warm wishes for the holidays. The cost of a stamp: two cents. The Baltimore Post Office moves over a million postcards through its doors during this Christmas season. And roughly 750,000 cards are handled by the St. Louis Post Office on a single day!

- **Burl Ives** is born this year. Decades later, he becomes the beloved narrator of *Rudolph the Red-Nosed Reindeer*, in which he sings such classics as "Silver Bells" and "A Holly Jolly Christmas."

- Children keep postal workers busy with lots of **letters to Santa**. What are among youngsters' most frequent requests? Well, not the Wii or iPods; instead, kids crave fruit and nuts! And it's a good thing, seeing the average weekly wage is $12.98.

Remembering the **1910s**

The most remarkable Christmas event of the decade occurred on World War I's Western Front in 1914, when British and German combatants emerged from the trenches to share songs, food, drink, and good will. Back in the States, mass production engendered new prosperity, and America, coming of age as a world power, began exporting its popular culture. Holiday celebrations during this "Ballroom Decade" featured the Fox Trot and Tango, while hot new toys for gifting included building sets Tinker Toys and Lincoln Logs, and the Ouija Board.

1910

An early film adaption of Charles Dickens's **A Christmas Carol** is released by Edison Studios. Directed by J. Searle Dawley, the silent film runs 15 minutes in length.

- **Neon lights are seen for the first time** at the Paris Auto Show on December 3.

- The **Brooklyn Cocktail** (usually containing rye, sweet vermouth, Amer Picon, and maraschino) is invented, livening many a holiday gathering in the "City of Kings" and elsewhere.

- Henry Ford opens the world's largest factory in Highland, Michigan, and the price of the **Model T** drops to $780—just in time for Christmas! *Vroom! Vroom!*

1911

"A MERRY CHRISTMAS."

Christmas cards often reflect the social climate; here, Santa gives **women the vote** (in California). Arizona and Kansas follow suit in 1912, although a constitutional amendment giving all American women the vote will not pass for years to come.

- With the promise of religious freedom (including the celebration of Christmas!) being one of America's chief attractions, it's no wonder immigrants flock here. 1911 is a banner year for **immigration**, with the Ellis Island record for numbers of immigrants processed set on April 17. On this day, 11,745 immigrants are processed—that's almost 500 people per hour, more than eight every minute!

The Irving Berlin classic song **"Alexander's Ragtime Band"** is published this year and becomes a huge hit; it's no doubt performed at more than a few holiday gatherings.

1912

Tiny Tim and Bob Cratchit
on Christmas Day

In came little Bob, the father, with at least three feet of comforter, exclusive of the fringe, hanging down before him; and his threadbare clothes darned up and brushed to look seasonable; and Tiny Tim upon his shoulder.

OCTOBER								NOVEMBER							DECEMBER					
Sun	Mon	Tue	Wed	Thur	Fri	Sat		Sun	Mon	Tue	Wed	Thur	Fri	Sat	Sun	Mon	Tue	Wed	Thur	Fri	Sat
	1	2	3	4	5								1	2	1	2	3	4	5	6	7
6	7	8	9	10	11	12		3	4	5	6	7	8	9	8	9	10	11	12	13	14
13	14	15	16	17	18	19		10	11	12	13	14	15	16	15	16	17	18	19	20	21
20	21	22	23	24	25	26		17	18	19	20	21	22	23	22	23	24	25	26	27	28
27	28	29	30	31				24	25	26	27	28	29	30	29	30	31				

- The nation's first municipal Christmas tree is dedicated in Madison Square Park, New York City, on December 23, introducing the tradition of **community Christmas trees**.

- It's a banner year for everyone with a sweet tooth. Prizes are added to **Cracker Jack** candy, **Crane's Peppermint Life Savers** make their debut, and National Biscuit Company (which later became Nabisco) introduces the **Oreo cookie**. All perfect stocking stuffers!

- J. Hartley Manners' ***Peg o' My Heart,*** a musical comedy featuring the popular song of the same name, debuts on December 20 in New York City's Cort Theatre and runs for 603 performances.

- Seattle's Bon Marche Department Store offers such gifts as **Hohner's Harmonica** (25 cents), the **Everlasting Spinning Top** (ten cents), and the **Goldsmith Football** (two dollars).

Featured in this 1912 calendar is **Jessie Willcox Smith's** illustration of *Tiny Tim and Bob Cratchit on Christmas Day*. Smith, a popular artist of the time, is best known for her work in magazines such as *Good Housekeeping* and *Ladies' Home Journal*.

1913

Workers prepare for the lighting of the **first National Christmas Tree** at the Capitol. President Woodrow Wilson presides over the event, which attracts an audience of 20,000, and features 1,000 singers and the U.S. Marine Band.

On December 1, the first **"drive-in" gas station** opens in Pittsburgh, current home of the Gulf Oil Company. The price for a gallon of gas? Eight cents!

The **first crossword puzzle** is published in the *New York World* days before Christmas, on December 21. Its creator: journalist Arthur Wynne.

- The Standard Candy Company of Nashville, Tennessee, invents its silly-sounding but delicious **Goo Goo Cluster**. The round-shaped treat, made of chocolate, caramel, peanuts, and marshmallow, is the first candy to combine ingredients in this way. It's still a favorite stocking stuffer throughout the South.

- The soon-to-be-iconic **Kewpie doll** makes her debut (and no doubt many appearances on little girls' letters to Santa). Early models are made of china, bisque, and celluloid.

- The **Erector Set** is invented by A. C. Gilbert. A must-have Christmas gift for young boys, it's said to be the first toy nationally advertised in America.

1914

Despite the start of World War I earlier this year, British and German soldiers on the Western Front suspend hostilities to celebrate yuletide during what becomes known as the **Christmas Truce.**

- Midgets dressed as elves introduce inventor Charles Pajeau's **Tinker Toys** as part of a Chicago department store window display. A set of the toys costs 60 cents. Their tube packaging remains relatively unchanged to this day.

- Popular entertainments for the Christmas season include Irving Berlin's musical revue *Watch Your Step* and the silent film comedy *Tillie's Punctured Romance*. Both open in December.

- Dedicated to the preservation of children's belief in Kris Kringle, the **Santa Claus Association** is founded by New York City philanthropists. Children's letters are delivered to the association, which provides gifts for needy children.

1915

Anywhere you find red-blooded soldiers you may expect racy images, and the holiday season is no exception. World War I British soldiers stationed in Cairo, Egypt, amuse themselves by exchanging **pin-up style holiday cards**.

- The Hallmark press, just five years old, is destroyed by fire. Its founders, the Hall brothers, rebuild it and introduce **Hallmark's first Christmas cards**.

- **Albert Einstein's** *General Theory of Relativity* is published on December 16.

- John B. Gruelle is granted a patent for the **Raggedy Ann doll** and it becomes a Christmas favorite. Legends surround the creation of this beloved toy, and a series of *Raggedy Ann* storybooks follow in 1918. Ann's brother, Raggedy Andy, is introduced in the 1920s.

- When **Henry Clay Frick** discovers that the failure of a Pittsburgh bank caused local children to lose their Christmas savings, he wires another bank and arranges to have the savings paid, though it cost him nearly $170,000.

1916

In the Land of Lincoln (Illinois), John Lloyd Wright, son of famous architect Frank Lloyd Wright, invents **Lincoln Logs**, which keep many young architects-to-be and other children busy constructing toy buildings on Christmas morning.

- The first **Piggly Wiggly** Grocery Store opens in Memphis, Tennessee, in September. Founded by Clarence Saunders, the innovative store introduced the concept of "self service" to busy shoppers preparing for Christmas parties and dinners.

- The Curtiss Candy Company is founded by Otto Schnering. Its first offering: the **Kandy Kake**, which filled stockings (and tummies!). The confection later evolved into the ever-popular Baby Ruth.

1917

Young Italian immigrant Antonio Pasin, apprenticed to a Chicago cabinetmaker, produces the first **Radio Flyer Wagon** (originally called the "Liberty Coaster"). The little red wagon becomes a Christmas favorite for decades. Here, the third generation of Pasins in the business pose in 1997.

- When a Hallmark shop in Kansas City sells out of sheets of red-and-green tissue paper, the shop's owner offers rolls of decorative envelope liners, selling them for ten cents each. An immediate hit with shoppers, the **gift wrap rolls** are sold at the bargain price of three sheets for 25 cents in 1918.

- **Women's suffrage** remains in the headlines; women in New York receive an early Christmas present by obtaining the right to vote in November.

- Just in time for Christmas, Father Edward Flanagan founds **Boys Town**, outside Omaha, Nebraska, in order to provide underprivileged boys an opportunity for a better life.

1918

Despite the growing popularity and affordability of the automobile, many people still depend on four-legged friends for transport. In rural America, it's common for a family to haul its Christmas tree home in the back of a **horse-drawn carriage**.

- Inventors Mabry Lovejoy and Joshua Kuykendall invent a **mechanical Santa Claus toy**. The ingenious toy is designed to be attached to a wall or other support. Santa's sleigh can be filled with gifts and treats, and stockings can be suspended from the team of reindeer.

- **Halifax, Nova Scotia,** begins a tradition of sending a large **Christmas tree to Boston** in gratitude for assistance after a devastating collision of two ships in Halifax Harbor the previous year, causing the deaths of almost 2,000 people, and the injury of about 4,000. The tree becomes an annual gift in 1971.

- **President Woodrow Wilson** becomes the first sitting president to travel abroad. He leaves on December 4 and is warmly greeted by the French, with whom he is very popular.

1919

- Librarian Ruth Abbott releases *A Suggestive List of Children's Books for Christmas*. Included on the list is *Aesop for Children*, illustrated by Milo Winter, which sells for two dollars.

- Avid readers hope to find Vicente Blasco Ibanez's bestselling novel *The Four Horsemen of the Apocalypse* under their trees. The cost? $1.90!

- The **Louis Marx Toy Company** is founded, launching decades of top-selling toys, including the Big Wheel and Rock 'Em Sock 'Em Robots. Louis Marx is sometimes called the "Henry Ford of the toy industry."

Remembering the **1920s**

The relief and prosperity that came with the end of World War I gave way to that decade of high spirits known as the Roaring Twenties. Correspondingly, the image of Santa Claus as a jolly, bearded, portly man in a red suit with white trim (created earlier by cartoonist Thomas Nast) was embraced by the masses. Some of America's favorite holiday traditions, such as the Macy's Thanksgiving Day Parade and Guy Lombardo's New Year's Eve broadcast, began in this decade. And the invention of suitable plastics helped the toy industry take off. Among youngsters' favorite gifts: pedal toys like fire trucks and farm tractors. Tiddlywinks, Pogo Sticks, teddy bears, train sets, and yo-yos were found under many Christmas trees as well.

1920

Thousands of World War I airplanes are converted to civilian use and **transcontinental air mail** service begins. Even Santa gets into the act in this biplane stunt!

- President Woodrow Wilson is awarded the **Nobel Peace Prize** in December for working to forge a lasting peace treaty and the League of Nations. His efforts pave the way for the United Nations.

- The 18th Amendment becomes law, **Prohibition** begins, and the most spirited of seasons is without spirits! Women across America receive a hard-won gift with the **19th Amendment** granting them the right to vote.

- Ellis Gimbel of department store fame begins the **first Thanksgiving Day Parade** in Philadelphia, a quickly adopted tradition that signifies the start of the holiday shopping season.

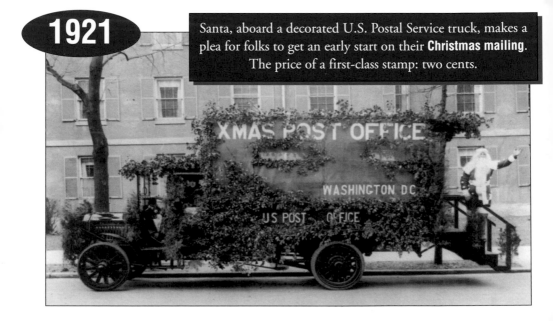

1921

Santa, aboard a decorated U.S. Postal Service truck, makes a plea for folks to get an early start on their **Christmas mailing**. The price of a first-class stamp: two cents.

- **Norman Rockwell's** painting, *Merrie Christmas,* appears on the December 3 cover of *The Saturday Evening Post.* Rockwell's art is hugely popular; this was his seventh cover of the year for the magazine.

- President Warren G. Harding issues the **Christmas Pardon of Eugene V. Debs**, a pacifist who was arrested after he delivered a famous antiwar speech in Canton, Ohio.

- The silent film ***The Little Minister***, released on Christmas Day, begins a tradition of seasonal flicks with holiday themes.

1922

I Knew He Would Come

PRAJER'S DRUG STORE
The Store with the Spirit of Christmas

Retailers get into the spirit of the season, as reflected by this ad for children's toys in a Colorado newspaper.

- General Electric discontinues its round Christmas light bulbs, and new **cone-shaped Christmas lights** (like the ones we use today) adorn homes and trees.

- Margery Williams' ***The Velveteen Rabbit*** is published and becomes an instant classic and favorite gift. In the story a velveteen rabbit, given to a young boy at Christmas, demonstrates the power of love.

- The Kaufman Brothers found a candy business that later becomes **KB Toys**, one of the largest toy retailers in the U.S. For decades before its demise (shortly before Christmas in 2008), KB offered inexpensive toys that stuffed many a stocking.

- **BBC Radio** begins daily broadcasts on December 23rd and airs the first British radio play, *Truth about Father Christmas*, the following day.

1923

President Calvin Coolidge lights the **National Christmas Tree** on Christmas Eve, beginning an annual tradition at the White House. Illuminated by 2,500 lights, the 48-foot balsam fir from Vermont lights up the Ellipse.

- **"The Charleston"** inspires the dance craze that will epitomize this decade of flappers and jazz. The song later features in the school dance scene of the classic Christmas movie *It's a Wonderful Life*.

- Paul Whiteman, the "King of Jazz," takes the Christmas tune **"Parade of the Wooden Soldiers"** to number one, signifying the fondness for high holiday spirits and jazz.

- Beatrice Alexander takes out a $1,600 loan to create the **Alexander Doll Company**, and her irresistible dolls climb to the tops of little girls' wish lists. More than eight decades later, those girls' great-great-granddaughters still enjoy playing with Madame Alexander's dolls.

- **Hasbro** is founded by the Hassenfeld Brothers, Henry and Helal. Originally a textile remnant company, Hasbro also produces pencil boxes and school supplies before becoming a toy giant. Mr. Potato Head was its first big hit in the fifties.

1924

The event that becomes the annual **Macy's Thanksgiving Day Parade** starts this year! Four hundred Macy's employees, dozens of animals from the Central Park Zoo, bands, and floats wind through New York City, with Santa Claus bringing up the rear.

- The American Forestry Association donates the first living Christmas tree for the **White House National Community Christmas Tree** ceremony, which is moved to Sherman Plaza.

- Christmas gets into the swing of the decade when rising star Louis Armstrong records **"Santa Claus Blues."**

- Iconic Saint Nick, increasingly embraced by popular culture, features as a red herring in the comic silent short film, *The Detective's Santa Claus*.

- **Frozen food,** a boon for busy shoppers, is invented by Clarence Birdseye!

1925

F. Scott Fitzgerald, wife, Zelda, and daughter, Scottie, celebrate Christmas in France, the year *The Great Gatsby* is published. With its themes of wealth and decadence, Fitzgerald's landmark novel is a testament to the excesses of the Roaring Twenties.

- The very first **Winnie-the-Pooh** story, "The Wrong Sort of Bees," is published on December 24. Author A. A. Milne goes on to write a series of books, illustrated by Ernest H. Shepard, featuring Pooh and his friends, some of the best-loved characters in children's literature.

- **Felix the Cat** is the feline's pajamas! Featured in a comic strip and in wildly popular animated films, Felix is also this year's top gift item. Felix the Cat dolls, toys, cigars, and clothing are snapped up all over North America and England.

- The Missouri Rockets, a precision dance team, makes its debut in St. Louis and becomes the basis for the Big Apple's **Rockettes**, who now entertain millions with their *Radio City Christmas Spectacular*.

1926

The stately **General Grant Tree**, a giant sequoia in King's Canyon National Park, California, is designated the "Nation's Christmas Tree" by President Calvin Coolidge. Object of an annual "Trek to the Tree" (the 80th Trek, in 2005, is pictured here), the 267-foot-tall sequoia is thought to be 1,650 years old.

- The world's first singing commercial, for Wheaties cereal, airs on the radio on Christmas Eve. Its four singers, eventually known as the **Wheaties Quartet,** were paid six dollars a week. The commercials were so successful that they are broadcast for the next six years.

- **Neiman Marcus's** famous "Christmas Book" mail-order catalog appears. The annual gift guide features increasingly fanciful items as the century unfolds, including Texas stadium end zone turf, personalized jetliners, and adult-sized robots.

- Wall Street **Christmas bonuses** skyrocket as the bull market encourages cash or stock dividends in this giddily profitable boom year. Wrote the *New York Times,* "Wall Street sees no disturbing clouds as it looks ahead to 1927."

1927

·WITH·BEST·WISHES·

Christmas postcards give way to cards with envelopes in the 1920s. A woodcut illustration by George Buday adorns this card.

- Large air- and helium-filled **balloons** begin making appearances in the **Macy's Thanksgiving Day Parade**. The first balloon: Felix the Cat, produced by the Goodyear Tire and Rubber Company.

- The invention of polystyrene makes strong **plastic toys** possible. Manufacturers take advantage of this new opportunity to produce dolls, models, and other toys more cheaply.

- **President Coolidge's Christmas message** is published in newspapers across the country: "Christmas is not a time or a season but a state of mind. To cherish peace and good will, to be plenteous in mercy, is to have the real spirit of Christmas."

- Finding an **electric toy train set** under the tree is the dream of many boys. This is a banner decade for toy trains, with Lionel and American Flyer big players. In 1927 the *Lionel Limited* passenger train cost $82.50, about a quarter of the price of Ford's newest Model T, listed at $360.

- **Charles Lindbergh** lands in Paris, completing the first solo non-stop trans-Atlantic flight. He becomes a huge celebrity on his return to the States, and souvenirs of his historic feat become hot gift items, from buttons and china to clothing and pillowcases.

1928

House Beautiful magazine, admired for its artistic covers, features busy Christmas shoppers on this 1928 issue. It will be a very different holiday shopping season next year, following the Great Crash of 1929.

- **Mickey Mouse** makes his first real star appearance on November 18 in *Steamboat Willie*, the first animation to feature synchronized sound effects and music. Mickey mania is in full swing by year's end with the release of short film *Gallopin' Gaucho* on December 30.

- After having been called "Santaclause," a **town in Indiana** officially changes its name back to **"Santa Claus."** But, after its Post Office is overwhelmed with holiday mail addressed to Santa, the Postal Service decides never to have another United States "Santa Claus" Post Office again!

1929

A **Captain Nemo** balloon makes its way along the Macy's Thanksgiving Day Parade route. This is the first year Macy's releases balloons at the parade's end, offering a reward for their return, a practice discontinued after an airplane pilot nearly crashes while trying to retrieve a balloon in 1932.

The **yo-yo** is introduced and a yo-yo craze ensues, with 300,000 made daily by year's end. The perfect stocking stuffer!

Canada's Guy Lombardo begins his annual live New Year's Eve broadcasts, popularizing the use of **"Auld Lang Syne"** for the occasion.

Remembering the **1930s**

Construction workers at the Rockefeller Center site *erected a makeshift Christmas tree in 1931, epitomizing the American spirit that persevered despite the Great Depression, when unemployment rose to 25 percent and the average family income dropped 40 percent. The demand for cheap entertainment made movies, radio shows, and board games popular, ushering in a golden age of stage and screen productions featuring such stars as Mickey Mouse, Rudolph the Red-Nosed Reindeer, Jack Benny, and Shirley Temple. When* Gone With the Wind *took the country by storm, Madame Alexander produced some of the first licensed dolls; her Scarlett O'Hara doll was on every girl's Christmas list. President Franklin Delano Roosevelt provided comfort and guidance, and Big Bands swept Americans off their feet during swinging holidays.*

1930

Mickey Mouse toys are extremely popular; shown here is a 1930 Mickey made by German toymaker Schuco.

- Before 1930, most Christmas trees grew wild in fields and forests. After, more and more trees are cultivated on **tree farms**. By the end of the century, approximately 36 million trees are harvested annually, and tree farming provides work for thousands of Americans.

- Need to get to Grandmother's house by car this Christmas? Gas costs **ten cents a gallon**. And Grandma's house itself costs approximately $7,145.

1931

Even during the Great Depression, the Christmas spirit inspires construction workers to erect a 20-foot balsam fir on the muddy site of what would become Rockefeller Center. Here they line up for their pay at the foot of the tree. **Rockefeller Center Christmas Trees** now attract visitors from around the world, although they are slightly taller! In fact, Rockefeller trees must be at least 65 feet high and 35 feet wide. The 1999 tree was the tallest at 100 feet.

- The **Coca-Cola Company** introduces its **first Santa** this year in *The Saturday Evening Post*, and the jolly old elf is an immediate success. Artist Haddon Sundblom continued painting a different Santa for the soft drink company each year through 1964. How much does a refreshing Coke cost Kris Kringle in 1931? A nickel!

- The short film, ***The Christmas Party***, starring Jackie Cooper, Norma Shearer, and Clark Gable, releases in December.

1932

- Many people believe the busiest shopping day of the year is the Friday after Thanksgiving. Actually, the Friday and Saturday before Christmas are the two **busiest shopping days of the year**.

- **The Jack Benny Program** radio show commences, and runs until 1948. One of its traditions: a "Christmas Shopping" episode, in which Benny purchases a cheap gift for announcer Don Wilson, has second thoughts, and returns the gift multiple times, driving his psychiatrist and wife crazy.

- After losing his job during the Great Depression, architect Alfred Butt invents ***Scrabble*** (originally called *Lexico*). Initially, he makes wooden game sets by hand and gives them to friends. When he pitches the game to big manufacturers, they turn him down. It isn't until the late 1940s and early 1950s that *Scrabble* takes off.

On December 8, 1933, FDR is presented with a collection of **Christmas Seals** by the National Tuberculosis Association. Christmas Seals were introduced to the United States by Emily Bissell in 1907.

- The **Rockefeller Center Christmas Tree** has its formal beginnings this year, when a tree is decorated with 700 lights and placed in front of the RCA Building.

- People flock to the magic of motion pictures to escape the Depression's gloom. For 25 cents, audiences enjoy such **holiday films** as *The Night Before Christmas* and *Making a Christmas Pudding,* featuring Tommy Handley.

- The Radio City Music Hall *Christmas Spectacular* premieres, featuring precision dance team, the **Rockettes**.

Six-year-old film star **Shirley Temple** realizes Santa Claus is fiction, not fact, when a department store Santa asks for her autograph. One of the year's most popular Christmas toys is the Shirley Temple Doll.

- **"Santa Claus Is Coming to Town"** is first sung on the radio on Eddie Cantor's show in November 1934. The next day, 100,000 orders for copies of its sheet music were placed. By Christmas, more than 400,000 copies of the song had been ordered.

- The song **"Winter Wonderland"** is published.

- Laurel and Hardy's version of **Babes in Toyland** is released on December 14.

1935

Monopoly is introduced in February of this year and becomes the most popular board game gift. Since its introduction, more than 200 million copies of *Monopoly* have sold worldwide. During World War II, games are sent to POW camps by British Intelligence; doctored boards are used to hide enemy currency, maps, files, and hacksaws.

Germany, Japan, and Czechoslovakia export over 250 million Christmas tree ornaments to the U.S. Later, Max Eckhardt, with the help of Corning Glass, brings the business of manufacturing **glass ornaments** to America.

The hilarious Marx Brothers/Kitty Carlisle film *A Night at the Opera* is released in November, providing audiences with sorely needed distraction. Movie goers also enjoy *Scrooge*.

1936

The **ice skating rink** at Rockefeller Plaza opens on Christmas Day, and eventually comes to attract 250,000 people each year.

- Animated short ***Christmas Comes but Once a Year*** is released on December 4.

- The **swing craze** is in, well, full swing! The Benny Goodman Trio, with Teddy Wilson on piano and Gene Krupa on drums, perform "Tiger Rag" and "You Turned the Tables on Me" on December 2.

1937

Czechoslovak Radio attempts an **incredible radio experiment** at 11PM on Christmas Eve, connecting three continents, with the country of India on the east and the United States on the west. Writer Karel Capek and inventor Frantisek Krizik from Czechoslovakia, poet Rabindranath Tagore in Bengal, and Albert Einstein in Princeton exchange good will messages at a time when the world was under the threat of war.

- MGM produces a three-minute color trailer featuring **Judy Garland** and the St. Luke's Episcopal Church Choristers of Long Beach, California, singing "Silent Night, Holy Night."

- It's believed that Irving Berlin writes **"White Christmas"** this holiday season during a stay at the Beverly Hills Hotel, when the composer is homesick for family and wintertime back east. It's said the song sat in a drawer for five years.

The classic **Spode Christmas tree** design, created by Harold Holdway, helps introduce the concept of Christmas-themed dinnerware to the U.S. The design continues to be the most collectible Christmas pattern in America.

- William Gruber invents the **View-Master 3D Viewer** as an educational tool. Instead, children prefer it as a toy! It remains with little change a popular present today, a testament to its originality.

- Another film version of **A Christmas Carol**, starring Reginald Owen and Gene Lockhart, entertains moviegoers this year. The average price of a ticket: 25 cents.

1939

Montgomery Ward gives copies of a story entitled ***Rudolph the Red-Nosed Reindeer***, written by employee Robert L. May, to customers' children as an advertising gimmick. It is set to music by Gene Autry in 1949. May is seen here with his family after Rudolph has become a hit!

- *Pow! Wham! Ka-zam!* Gotham City hero **Batman** makes his debut, and the comic book becomes one of the top Christmas gifts of the year.

- Retailer Fred Lazarus persuades FDR to change **Thanksgiving** from the last Thursday of November to the fourth Thursday of the month, creating a slightly longer **shopping season**.

- Across the country, over 60 million moviegoers anxiously await the release of ***Gone With the Wind*** on December 19. The excitement and accolades the film receives are never matched again.

- The **first live radio broadcast** of Dickens's ***A Christmas Carol*** airs on Christmas Eve; it's performed by Lionel Barrymore and narrated by Orson Welles.

Remembering the **1940s**

World War II mobilized and united America in the forties, with Bob Hope's USO Christmas tours lifting GI morale around the world and "I'll Be Home for Christmas" a holiday hit for those near and far away. War bonds were a popular gift, and Macy's Thanksgiving Day Parade was suspended in support of the war. But while America rolled up her sleeves during the first half of the decade, she let loose in the second, emerging as a world superpower. With civil rights and women's rights making headway, and college an option for most, gifts under the tree—including a new generation of toys—were more plentiful. The jitterbug livened dance floors everywhere. And Hollywood thrived, producing, among other flicks, the beloved Christmas classics It's a Wonderful Life *and* Miracle on 34th Street.

1940

In London, whole families celebrate Christmas in **Underground stations**, sheltered from night-long Nazi bombing raids.

Lighting the White House Christmas tree,
President Franklin Delano Roosevelt says that,
"by our works, as well as our words, we will strive forth
in faith and in hope and in love." He also requests that
the holiday be made merry for the children.

- **Nylon stockings** are introduced. Made of the first "miracle fabric," they become a favorite Christmas gift for women.

- Noma produces a **star with glass rays**, giving the effect of neon, for the top of the Christmas tree.

- Kodak makes a great Christmas present, a **35-millimeter high-speed camera** that sells for $14.50. Its folding camera sells for just $8.50.

- The **Ice Capades**, brainchild of impresario John H. Harris, debuts in Hershey, Pennsylvania.

- **Christmas films** include *Christmas in July*, with Dick Powell and Ellen Drew, and *Beyond Christmas*, with Harry Carey, C. Aubrey Smith, Charles Winninger, Jean Parker, and Richard Carlson.

1941

Even after the devastation of the **Pearl Harbor** attacks on December 7, shoppers try to maintain their Christmas spirit, as seen in a Woolworth's 5-and-dime store.

- **Bob Hope** performs his **first USO (United Service Organizations) show** for U.S. troops in California. He completes 60 world tours over the ensuing 50 years.

Inexpensive **model plane kits** made of plastic rather than balsa wood are introduced in the early 1940s, and boys start adding them to wish lists.

- The price of a **Christmas movie ticket** (as little as ten cents in some places) includes a double feature, a newsreel, one or more cartoons, and an adventure serial with a cliffhanger ending!

- An early Tom and Jerry cartoon, ***The Night Before Christmas***, and comedy film ***Sullivan's Travels*** are released in time for Christmas.

1942

The Irving Berlin song "Happy Holiday" is first sung by Bing Crosby in the film *Holiday Inn*, which also stars Fred Astaire, here performing his firecracker dance. Bing Crosby's recording of "White Christmas," also from *Holiday Inn*, becomes one of the bestselling records of all time.

- The first recording of "**'Twas the Night before Christmas**" as a song is made by Fred Waring.

- Subscribers to *The New Yorker* looked forward to its Christmas covers every year. The December 19 issue this year shows a Christmas tree being carried home on a bicycle.

- **Little Golden Books** come on the market at just 25 cents each, work their way into children's hearts, and become favorite Christmas presents for years to come. Later titles include *Rudolph the Red-Nosed Reindeer* and *Frosty the Snowman*.

1943

This Christmas—
GIVE WAR BONDS

THE GENERAL TIRE & RUBBER COMPANY • AKRON, OHIO

The Government recommends giving **War Bonds** for Christmas, and children buy war stamps in school.

- An early experimental television broadcast of Dickens's *A Christmas Carol* takes place.

- Bing Crosby records "**I'll Be Home for Christmas**" in October; it becomes the most-requested song during USO shows this yuletide.

- In Italy, **American GIs** drape Christmas trees with C-ration foil.

- Troops aboard the U.S.S. *North Carolina* mail a large check to **R. H. Macy and Company**, requesting the manager send appropriate gifts to their children back home.

1944

During World War II, **American GIs** cheer the children of a war-torn Italian village with Christmas presents.

- Servicemen and women away from home are often able to spend Christmas at a USO (United Service Organizations) or canteen, with volunteers serving and entertaining them. **The Hollywood Canteen** is staffed with movie stars, who wait on tables, serve food, wash dishes, and perform.

- Home bakers begin using margarine instead of butter, which is rationed, for **Christmas baking**. (Sugar, tires, and gasoline have already been rationed.)

- Homes have rooms with **blackout shades**. Nightly blackouts prevent enemy planes from focusing on targets. At Christmas, **outdoor carolers sing** without lighting of any kind—including candles!

- **Liquid leg makeup** replaces women's nylon stockings. Nylon is in short supply—it's needed for parachutes!

- The song **"Have Yourself a Merry Little Christmas"** cheers people during the war.

1945

The **Macy's Thanksgiving Day Parade** resumes this year, after its suspension in 1941 because of World War II.

- One of the most popular toys of the year is the **Slinky**, produced by James Industries. Slinky toys sold since would wrap around the world 126 times!

- It is a very merry Christmas this year— **World War II has ended**! Servicemen and women return home to greetings of joy.

- Films *The Bells of St. Mary's*, with Bing Crosby and Ingrid Bergman, and *Christmas in Connecticut* are high points of the season. "Let It Snow" and "Blue Christmas" are popular songs.

1946

The beloved movie *It's a Wonderful Life* premieres on December 20 in New York City. It's now shown on television every year at Christmas time.

- The first **Tupperware** is sold in department and hardware stores, and makes it a snap to store Christmas dinner leftovers!

- Now that the war is over, Christmas celebrations grow grander, and lighting companies offer exciting new effects. **Noma's "Bubble Lites"** become the world's best-selling Christmas tree decorations.

- **"The Christmas Song"** is recorded by the Nat King Cole Trio. The rendition gives everyone warm visions of "Chestnuts roasting on an open fire."

1947

Babe Ruth hits a home run with children afflicted by infantile paralysis when he dresses up as Santa Claus at a December 10 party given by the Sister Kenny Foundation.

- Christian Dior introduces its **New Look,** no doubt a popular choice for many women attending holiday parties!

Toys for Tots organizes its first Christmas toy drive for needy children.

- One of New York's **heaviest recorded snowfalls** (26.4 inches) occurs the day after Christmas.

- Flying becomes more affordable, and civilian **air travel** grows from 2.5 million passengers in 1937 to 21 million in 1947. Many are now able to take Christmas vacations far from home.

- Children love the movie ***Miracle on 34th Street***, with Edmund Gwenn as Kris Kringle and Natalie Wood as the little girl who meets the real Santa Claus. Adults are entertained by the fantasy *The Bishop's Wife*.

- Gene Autry records **"Here Comes·Santa Claus,"** his first holiday song; it's an instant hit.

1948

Kiss Me, Kate
premieres on Broadway
on December 30.
Cole Porter's most
successful musical,
the production runs for
1,077 performances.

- The name of word game *Lexico* is officially changed to **Scrabble,** and sales take off.

- The first commercial **long-playing record (LP)** is introduced this year; it allows listeners to hear 23 minutes of music without interruption. Stereophonic sound also gives so-called high fidelity to recordings. One of the songs folks enjoy on their record players this yuletide: *"All I Want for Christmas Is My Two Front Teeth,"* recorded by Spike Jones and his City Slickers!

- Holiday moviegoers enjoy *3 Godfathers* with John Wayne and *Joan of Arc* starring Ingrid Bergman; the actress is nominated for an Academy Award for her performance.

1949

Originally called "Automatic Binding Bricks,"
LEGO blocks are manufactured by a Danish toy
maker and become a Christmas favorite.

Board games always make good Christmas gifts; what better way to keep the kids busy Christmas morning? Popular games this year: *Candy Land*, considered a child's first game, and *Clue*, the "whodunit" murder mystery game, originally called *Cluedo*.

- **UNICEF** produces the first charity Christmas card. Its image of children dancing around a maypole is painted by a seven-year-old Czechoslovakian girl; the picture represents "joy going round and round."

Johnny Marks writes the song
"Rudolph the Red-Nosed Reindeer."
It's recorded by Gene Autry and becomes his all-time bestseller as well as the second most popular Christmas song of all time, after **"White Christmas."**

- **"It's a Marshmallow World"** is written by Carl Sigman and Peter DeRose. The song is recorded in 1950 by Bing Crosby. Margaret Whiting and Johnny Mercer team up to sing Frank Loesser's **"Baby, It's Cold Outside;"** their recording becomes the most heard version of this song.

Remembering the **1950s**

As Baby Boomers toddled and jived their way through the fifties, the toy industry responded to the enormous market and new prosperity with a cornucopia of "firsts." From hula hoops, Barbie dolls, and Play-Doh to Matchbox cars and Silly Putty, wonderful novelty toys provided a bumper yield under the new aluminum Christmas trees. Americans were introduced to Bing Crosby's "White Christmas" and George Balanchine's The Nutcracker, *as well as to portable television sets, Disneyland, and Campbell's Green Bean Casserole. Mr. Potato Head, the first toy advertised on TV, topped many a Christmas wish list. The holiday rocked to the tunes of "I Saw Mommy Kissing Santa Claus," "Santa Baby," "Jingle Bell Rock," and December 25, 1958's Number 1 hit, "The Chipmunk Song."*

1950

- The Addis Brush Company introduces the **"Silver Pine" aluminum Christmas tree**. It consists of an aluminum cone illuminated by a rotating color disk and a projected light. Originals are now considered collector's items.

- Every American boy wants an **electric train set** for Christmas. Prices range from $15.95 to $69.95; compare with today's $239.95!

- **Perry Como** records "The Story of the First Christmas."

- The *Howdy Doody* children's program is used by TV maker RCA to sell color television sets.

- **Silly Putty** is introduced and becomes a favorite family stocking stuffer.

- Among the top **Christmas songs** this year: "There Is No Christmas like a Home Christmas," "Frosty the Snowman," "Sleigh Ride," "Silver Bells," and especially Bing Crosby's record of "Christmas in Killarney."

1951

Motorola produces a **14-inch television set**, called the first large-screen portable set, just in time for the Christmas shopping season.

- The film *A Christmas Carol*, starring Alastair Sim, is released. This version of Dickens's tale is considered among the best ever made.

- Gene Autry records **"Frosty the Snowman."**

- Among the **Christmas presents sent to President Harry S. Truman** at the White House this year: a book entitled *Guide to Confident Living*, a two-pound fruitcake, 60 razor blades, Vermont maple syrup, suspenders, bourbon, wool socks, potatoes, and a donkey!

- The Christmas classic ***Amahl and the Night Visitors***, a one-act opera by Gian Carlo Menotti, is commissioned by NBC and broadcast live on December 24. It's the first Hallmark Hall of Fame production, and the first opera composed specifically for American television.

- **"It's Beginning to Look a Lot like Christmas,"** by Meredith Willson is an appropriate song for the season.

1952

At its toy and doll show in December, the **Henry Ford Museum** presents contrasting toy versions of a modern car and a 1927 Model "T," driven here by young enthusiasts.

- Americans meet **Mr. Potato Head**. The spudsation, originally intended to be used with a real potato, is the first toy advertised on television, taking it to the top of many kids' wish lists.

- The December issue of ***The American Home*** offers instructions for making footstools from fruit cans.

- Walt Disney entrances youngsters with the Mickey Mouse cartoon ***Pluto's Christmas Tree***.

- **Queen Elizabeth's** first Christmas radio message is broadcast live from Sandringham.

- New **Christmas songs** this year include "I Saw Mommy Kissing Santa Claus," "The Night Before Christmas Song," and "Nuttin' for Christmas," a humorous number for children.

1953

President Dwight D. Eisenhower consults with the president of Hallmark to produce the first **White House Christmas cards**—they feature Ike's own artwork!

Matchbox cars are introduced, driving boys everywhere to add the miniature vehicles to their Christmas lists.

Eartha Kitt's recording of **"Santa Baby"** is a suggestive seasonal number for adults, while Louis Armstrong's **"Zat You, Santa Claus?"** and **"Cool Yule"** add soul to the season.

As seen here in 1953, four years after its opening, New York City's **Wollman Rink** continues to attract merry ice-skaters!

1954

White Christmas, with Bing Crosby and Danny Kaye, is the first film made in VistaVision, a format that afforded larger, brighter, and less fuzzy images.

- *Frosty the Snowman* appears as an animated, made-for-TV short.

- The New York City Ballet gives its first performance of **George Balanchine's** *The Nutcracker*.

- Kids want walking, remote-controlled **Robert the Robot** for Christmas.

- "Caroling, Caroling" and **Perry Como's** recording of "There's No Place like Home for the Holidays" are hits with those who favor traditional songs; "The Christmas Waltz" is enjoyed for its jazzy style.

1955

Campbell's famous **Green Bean Casserole**, featuring Cream of Mushroom Soup, makes its debut and becomes a holiday dinner mainstay.

- Open this year: **Disneyland**, the Walt Disney theme park. The park celebrates yuletide with its first Christmas event, "Christmas Around the World."

- The **Madame Alexander Doll Cissy**, called the first modern fashion doll, is noted for her womanly figure and high heels.

- Edgy Christmas comedy ***We're No Angels*** is the movie hit of the season. Its all-star cast includes Humphrey Bogart, Peter Ustinov, and Joan Bennett.

1956

Play-Doh is introduced. Originally intended to be wallpaper cleaner, the non-toxic, mess-free modeling compound is a big hit with parents, who soon make it a top-selling Christmas gift.

- **Mamie Eisenhower** shops for White House staff gifts and wraps them herself, an unusual thing for a First Lady to do.

- ***Household*** magazine shows how to make a tabletop Christmas tree out of Styrofoam balls and glitter-dipped toothpicks.

- Prolific composer **Johnny Marks** produces two Christmas songs in 1956: "Everyone's a Child at Christmas" and "I Heard the Bells on Christmas Day."

1957

A decorated horse-drawn carriage, advertising a local store, travels down **New York's Fifth Avenue**. In the photograph's background: Saks Fifth Avenue and St. Patrick's Cathedral.

- The Dr. Seuss book, *How the Grinch Stole Christmas*, is published.
- **Queen Elizabeth's annual Christmas speech** is televised for the first time this year.
- The songs **"Jingle Bell Rock"** and **"Let's Light the Christmas Tree"** are released in time for Christmas. The latter, initially a regional favorite in the Cincinnati area, gains enough national popularity to become one of the top 100 records in December's *Billboard*.

1958

- Bobs Candies, producer of **peppermint candy canes**, refines a machine first developed by Father Harding Keller, family member and Catholic priest, to automatically bend the candy cane, thereby streamlining production.
- **First Lady Mamie Eisenhower** orders 27 decorated Christmas trees for the White House.
- **"The Chipmunk Song"** becomes the only Christmas song in American history to be number one on December 25.
- **"Rockin' around the Christmas Tree"** and **"The Little Drummer Boy"** are among the other popular songs this season.
- **Balanchine's *The Nutcracker*** ballet is shown on prime-time television in color for the first time.
- A recorded Christmas message by **President Dwight D. Eisenhower** is the first voice heard from space. Said Ike, "To all mankind, America's wish for Peace on Earth and Good Will to Men Everywhere."

The young and young-at-heart have a cool yule shakin' their hips with the brand new WHAM-O **Hula Hoop**! More than 25 million are made in this, its first year.

1959

A seamstress takes final measurements for **Rockette costumes** at Radio City Music Hall.

The **Barbie doll** is introduced;
in a few years it becomes one of the
Christmas gifts most requested by girls.

Neiman Marcus continues to offer unique gifts
in its famous Christmas catalog. This year you can order
a Black Angus steer, delivered live or in steaks!

Better Homes & Gardens magazine features
instructions for crafting homemade toy soldiers
and dolls from thread spools, pipe cleaners,
and other household items.

Wisconsin's Aluminum Specialty Company
begins manufacturing **aluminum Christmas trees**.
They are now collector's items.

Johnny Marks pens two Christmas songs this year:
"A Merry, Merry Christmas to You"
and "The Santa Claus Parade."

Remembering the **1960s**

The sixties heralded America's first Christmas stamps, Sidewalk Santas, "A Holly Jolly Christmas," and Easy-Bake Ovens. Elvis was in the army and men landed on the moon. But it was also a time of conflict, change, and assassination—JFK's death on November 22, 1963, made for a grim holiday that year. Where the Wild Things Are *became a childhood classic, sharing space under the tree with Etch-A-Sketch and Twister. Popular TV specials*—A Charlie Brown Christmas, How the Grinch Stole Christmas, *and* Rudolph the Red-Nosed Reindeer—*emphasized the reason for the season, appealing to a sense of innocence and good will in the midst of upheaval.*

1960

- The book *Nine Days to Christmas*, illustrated by Marie Hall Ets, is awarded the Caldecott Medal, the award for the year's most distinguished American picture book for children.

- The Ohio Art Company introduces **Etch-A-Sketch** to the American marketplace. Television advertising creates an enormous demand for the drawing toys, and they're produced right up until Christmas Eve, with Ohio Art shipping them overnight to arrive on Christmas Day.

- On December 26, the musical *Do Re Mi* with Phil Silvers premieres in New York City at the St. James Theatre. It runs for 400 performances.

Elvis returns from Germany early this year after serving one and one half years in the Armed Services. His recording of "Are You Lonesome Tonight?" becomes number one on November 28, and stays atop the *Billboard* charts for six weeks. Presley is seen here at home in Memphis.

1961

Young Caroline Kennedy trims a festive White House Christmas tree. On December 9, her father, John F. Kennedy, proclaims December 10–17 **Human Rights Week**.

- **Scotch Brand Magic Transparent Tape** is invented. The almost invisible tape seals countless Christmas packages placed under holiday trees.

- A Disney Technicolor film version of Christmas musical **Babes in Toyland**, based on Victor Herbert's 1903 operetta, is released on December 14.

The Sidewalk Santa program increases in popularity in the 1960s. The first **Sidewalk Santas** (in 1900 Los Angeles) were actually jailed for creating a public nuisance! Protesters demonstrated for their release, and the group went on to raise $800 for Christmas dinners for the homeless and poor. The program continues today through Volunteers of America.

- The Post Office issues America's **first Christmas stamp**.

- The **world's largest Santa statue** is constructed for the Seattle World's Fair. The 42-foot-tall Saint Nick stood on an eight-foot base. If you'd like to visit him, you'll need to travel to his present home: the North Pole (naturally), Alaska!

- Johnny Marks writes **"A Holly Jolly Christmas."** It's first recorded by the Quinto Sisters, and later Burl Ives.

1963

- Hasbro introduces its **Easy-Bake Oven**, which sells for $15.95. A popular item on many youngsters' wish lists, the working toy oven sells over 500,000 in its first year.

- **The Beatles record their first Christmas greeting**, a special single for members of their official fan club. The tradition continues through 1969.

- Seasonal songs: **"Christmas (Baby Please Come Home)"** is released by Darlene Love. Roy Orbison records Willie Nelson's **"Pretty Paper;"** it becomes a Top 20 hit. **"It's the Most Wonderful Time of the Year,"** by Edward Pola and George Wyle, is recorded by Andy Williams.

- Christmas 1963 is a somber one; just one month after the assassination of **John F. Kennedy**. Still, people try to move forward as best they can, and honor the season.

1964

- Hess Corporation starts selling **Hess toy trucks** this Christmas. They continue to introduce a new model each year.

- On December 10, **Martin Luther King, Jr.** becomes the youngest man to receive the Nobel Peace Prize.

- Elvis's **"Blue Christmas"** becomes number one. Fittingly, the star for many years had decorated Graceland with blue Christmas lights.

Top TV special ***Rudolph the Red-Nosed Reindeer,*** produced by Rankin/Bass, airs for the first time on December 6. In addition to its namesake song, it features other soon-to-be-favorites, such as "A Holly Jolly Christmas," "Silver and Gold," "We Are Santa's Elves," and "Jingle, Jingle, Jingle."

1965

The Peanuts characters win our hearts when the animated television show *A Charlie Brown Christmas* premieres on December 9 and becomes an instant holiday classic.

PEANUTS © Peanuts Worldwide LLC

- The Supremes' *Merry Christmas* album is released in November. It includes favorite traditional songs as well as two original tunes.

- The **Super Ball** is invented by Norman Stingley and manufactured by WHAM-O. By Christmas it bounces its way into more than seven million homes.

1966

Pope Paul VI makes a Christmas visit to the city of Florence, Italy, which was devastated just one month earlier by one of its worst floods in history. The pontiff delivers gifts to children and holds a Christmas Mass.

- The Grinch discovers the true meaning of Christmas in *How the Grinch Stole Christmas*, which airs on television for the first time.

- The Beatles release **"Everywhere It's Christmas"** in the U.K. on December 16.

- The song **"We Need a Little Christmas"** by Jerry Herman is heard for the first time in the Broadway show *Mame*.

- Johnny Marks continues to make his mark in the world of Christmas songs with the release of **"A Caroling We Go."**

- Popular gifts this year include the **Spirograph**, **Rock 'Em Sock 'Em Robots**, and **Twister** (which was deemed by some toy industry competitors as "sex in a box" because it used human bodies as playing pieces).

Doctor Christiaan Barnard performs the world's **first human heart transplant** on December 3. He is seen here (*center*) on Christmas Eve with two other heart surgeons on the TV program *Face the Nation*.

- Hasbro introduces the **Lite Brite** toy, which lights up Christmas morning for many boys and girls.

- The ***Queen Mary*** ends its 30-year reign as a British luxury ocean liner, completing its final voyage on December 9.

1968

On Christmas Eve, astronauts Frank Borman, Jim Lovell, and William Anders become the **first humans to orbit the moon.** They transmit this image of Earth and read excerpts from the Book of Genesis to an estimated one billion people tuning in to the broadcast. Borman finished by saying, "And from the crew of *Apollo 8*, we close with good night, good luck, a Merry Christmas, and God bless all of you—all of you on the good Earth."

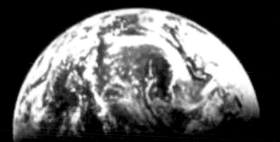

- **Mattel's Hot Wheels** toy cars are launched with 16 different designs—just in time to zoom their way into Christmas stockings!

- The Broadway musical ***Promises, Promises*** debuts December 1, and stars Jerry Orbach (of *Law and Order* fame). His role garners him a Tony Award for Best Actor in a Musical.

1969

The Rankin/Bass animated feature ***Frosty the Snowman*** melts our hearts when it airs for the first time on CBS. Jimmy Durante and Jackie Vernon lend their voices to the production.

- Billionaire **Ross Perot** attempts to deliver 28 tons of Christmas gifts and medicine to **American POWs** in North Vietnam, in a chartered jet that bears the message "Peace on Earth."

- Johnny Marks writes **"Joyous Christmas."**

Remembering the **1970s**

The kaleidoscopic seventies swirled with dramatic political events. John Lennon's "Happy Christmas (War Is Over)" song precedes Nixon's Christmas Bombing of North Vietnam the following year, which shocked Americans. Beleaguered by Watergate, Nixon would resign a year before the war's end in 1975. On the lighter side, Albert Finney's 1970 portrayal of Scrooge wins him the Golden Globe, and a cultural craze is kicked off by a movie that began "A long time ago in a galaxy far, far away. ..." Yuletide was celebrated to the beat of José Feliciano's "Feliz Navidad," "Merry Christmas, Darling," and yes, "Grandma Got Run Over by a Reindeer." Hallmark Keepsake Ornaments and Pet Rocks became hot collectibles, and Nerf balls, Dungeons and Dragons, The Snowman *picture book, and fledgling video games were holiday hits.*

1970

Albert Finney plays **Scrooge** in the film of the same name, based on Charles Dickens's *A Christmas Carol*, and wins a Golden Globe for his performance. The musical was also nominated for four Oscars.

- Parker Brothers introduces the "world's first official indoor ball," the **Nerf ball**. The foam ball is guaranteed not to break any windows Christmas morning! It sells an estimated four million units its first year.

- The animated film ***Santa Claus Is Comin' to Town*** airs on television December 14. Fred Astaire narrates the film; Mickey Rooney provides the voice of Kris Kringle.

- **The Carpenters** record the single **"Merry Christmas, Darling"** on November 20. Written by Richard Carpenter and Frank Pooler, it becomes number one on the *Billboard* Christmas singles chart this year, next year, and in 1973.

- Singer-songwriter **José Feliciano** writes "Feliz Navidad."

1971

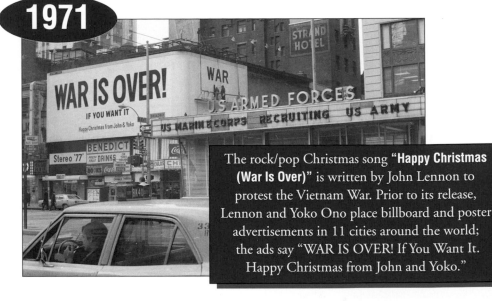

The rock/pop Christmas song **"Happy Christmas (War Is Over)"** is written by John Lennon to protest the Vietnam War. Prior to its release, Lennon and Yoko Ono place billboard and poster advertisements in 11 cities around the world; the ads say "WAR IS OVER! If You Want It. Happy Christmas from John and Yoko."

- Cuba bans Christmas celebrations. In defiance, Cuban Americans begin the **Three Kings' Day parade** in Miami.

- To the dismay of wives across America, **the longest game in NFL history** is played on Christmas Day. After 82 minutes and amidst the second overtime, Miami beats Kansas City in the AFC playoff.

- At the White House, **a special tree honoring POWs and MIAs** stands before the National Community Christmas Tree.

1972

Magnavox's *Odyssey*, the first video game machine, is one of the season's most popular gifts; it features a primitive form of paddle ball.

Santa Claus, Indiana, receives more than half a million letters and requests at Christmas. A first-class stamp costs eight cents.

President Nixon orders the **Christmas Bombing** of North Vietnam on December 18.

1973

The December 9 TV special, ***Bing Crosby's Sun Valley Christmas Show***, features Bing, wife Kathryn, and children Harry, Nathaniel, and Mary Frances.

- ***Dungeons and Dragons*** becomes one of the season's most sought-after games. Created by Dave Ameson and Gary Gygax, D&D is a fantasy/adventure RPG (role-playing game). Eventually, it's played worldwide, generating an approximately $250 million market.

- Six glass ball ornaments and 12 yarn figures become the first **Hallmark Keepsake Ornaments**. Unique in design, year-dated, and available for a limited time, the ornaments create a new collectible market.

- An October **oil embargo** by the organization now known as OPEC cuts oil supply and elevates fuel prices to levels never thought possible. Gas supplies are limited and drivers form long lines at gas stations for fuel, often in vain. Due to the energy crisis, the National Christmas Tree—a living Colorado blue spruce—is decorated in an energy-efficient manner.

- The International Society of Santa Claus gives **Johnny Marks and Irving Berlin** its Spirit of Christmas Award.

1974

- Horror movie *Black Christmas* creeps out audiences; it was made four years before *Halloween*, supposedly the first flick of the slasher genre.

- After several years of minimal snowfall, the residents of North St. Paul, Minnesota, decide to build a permanent snowman that wouldn't require any snow! Made of concrete, he becomes the **world's largest stucco snowman** at 54 feet.

- **Cyclone Tracy** devastates Darwin, Australia, on Christmas Eve. Neighboring communities commence fundraising and relief efforts immediately, with the town of Alice Springs raising over $105,000 by Christmas night. The catastrophe influences singer/songwriter Bill Cate to compose "Santa Never Made it into Darwin," which he performs with Boyd Robinson to raise money for cyclone victims.

1975

First Lady Betty Ford adorns the White House Christmas tree for the second time. She spent her first Christmas in the White House four months after Richard Nixon resigned as President of the United States in 1974.

- Werner Erhard of San Francisco, California, mails **62,824 Christmas cards**, using first-class stamps which cost 13 cents each. If he were to send the same number of cards 25 years later, it would cost over $20,000!

- The **Pet Rock**, brainchild of California salesman Gary Dahl, is an ideal pet, as it does not need much care! Each comes packaged in a gift box that looks like a pet carrying case. By Christmas, Dahl sells two and a half tons of rocks!

- Sears earns an exclusive deal to sell **Atari's *Home Pong*** video games. Over 150,000 units are sold during the Christmas season.

1976

Animated short ***The Little Drummer Boy Book II***, directed by Rankin/Bass, airs on NBC on December 13. Greer Garson is the storyteller and Zero Mostel plays Brutus.

Traveling by car over the river and through the woods to grandmother's house? Gas costs **59 cents a gallon**.

Fiddler on the Roof, starring Zero Mostel, opens on Broadway on December 28.

The revving of engines is heard across the country on Christmas morning, thanks to the "r-r-r" sounds produced by **R-R-R-Raw Power**. Attach the toy handle to your bike to create that super cool "revving" sound!

1977

The movie *Star Wars* premieres on May 25. By Christmas, it's such a phenomenon George Lucas's toy making partner Kenner sells 600,000 empty "IOU" action figure boxes.

December TV specials *A Flintstone Christmas*, Jim Henson's *Emmet Otter's Jug-Band Christmas*, and the *Johnny Cash Christmas Special* attract large viewing audiences.

- Milton Bradley's marble-munching board game, ***Hungry Hungry Hippos***, is a popular present.

- Wordless picture book ***The Snowman*** by Raymond Briggs is published, and becomes an instant Christmas classic. It becomes an animated 1982 movie that is broadcast each year.

- The Rankin/Bass version of *A Christmas Carol*, called ***The Stingiest Man in Town***, airs on TV on December 23.

The TV special *John Denver and the Muppets, A Christmas Together* airs on December 5. Denver sings "Silent Night" with backup vocals by Kermit the Frog, Miss Piggy, Fozzie Bear, and other Muppets.

- To remember the **hostages in Iran**, President Carter's daughter Amy lights only the tops of the National Christmas Tree and the surrounding state trees. Carter says, "We will turn on the rest of the lights when the hostages come home."

- Grandma drinks a little too much eggnog and becomes star of the Randy Brooks song **"Grandma Got Run Over by a Reindeer,"** performed by Elmo and Patsy Shropshire.

- Two **Christmas movies** shown on TV during this holiday season: *An American Christmas Carol* and *Christmas Lilies of the Field*.

Remembering the **1980s**

Christmas may have been a bit flashier during the materialistic eighties, with the stock market booming and halls decked to the hilt. Americans shopped till they dropped, phoned home, played Pictionary, triple dog-dared each other, and celebrated the December 1989 dismantling of the Berlin Wall. Santa brought a sleighful of colorful characters for under the tree, including Smurfs, Gremlins, Transformers, Masters of the Universe, Pound Puppies, and Cabbage Patch Dolls. Yuletides were made more fun by E.T. toys, Rubik's Cubes, and "Super Mario World," but the spirit of the season resonated to The Polar Express, the heartwarming children's book about the power of belief.

1980

- **Rubik's Cube**, invented by Hungarian Erno Rubik, comes to the U.S. Worldwide, 160 million are sold until 1982, when the puzzle market collapses. It takes another 15 years for the cube to again become popular.

- **Campbell's Soup** produces Christmas tree ornaments showing the Campbell Kids.

- Children love **Richard Scarry books**; Random House publishes his *Best Christmas Book Ever* in September. Scarry's books sell over 100 million copies and are translated into 30 languages.

- The following **Christmas films** were enjoyed by children during the holiday season: *Mr. Krueger's Christmas*, *A Snow White Christmas*, *Yogi's First Christmas*, *Pinocchio's Christmas*, and *The Christmas Raccoons*.

1981

The Smurfs, originally created in Belgium, are brought to North America by William Hanna and Joseph Barbera. The Saturday morning cartoon, a huge success, runs until 1990, and wins many awards. The sky-blue Smurfs also become stuffed animals many children put on their Christmas lists!

- *For Those About to Rock* by AC/DC becomes the number one album in the U.S. Released on November 23, it sells more than four million copies.

1982

Toys based on Steven Spielberg's movie *E.T.* are out-of-this-world bestsellers. Here the manager of F.A.O. Schwarz holds the last **E.T. toy** in the store on December 10.

- **President Ronald Reagan** delivers a Christmas Day address, and mentions receiving holiday greetings from U.S. Marines on peacekeeping duty in Beirut, Lebanon, and from a sailor on the U.S.S. *Enterprise* in the Indian Ocean.

- The Dustin Hoffman/Jessica Lange film **Tootsie**, released on December 17, is a must-see during the holiday season. Lange won an Oscar for Best Supporting Actress.

1983

The Red Ryder BB gun shown is the inspiration for **A Christmas Story**, a film based on Jean Shepherd's recollections of his Indiana childhood. The movie opens just before Thanksgiving, and becomes one of America's most popular Christmas movies.

- ABC TV begins airing ***Mickey's Once Upon a Christmas Parade*** at Disney's Magic Kingdom as a Christmas Day special.
- ***Trading Places***, starring Eddie Murphy, Dan Aykroyd, and Jamie Lee Curtis, is a popular movie during the holiday season. It's later nominated for an Academy Award for Best Comedy.
- The cuddly **Care Bears** stuffed toys come onto the Christmas scene.

1984

Pound Puppies are greeted with joy by boys and girls. They have floppy ears and droopy eyes, come with an adoption certificate, and are considered one of the holiday season's bestselling toys.

The warmest day for **Christmas Tree Lighting** on the White House lawn is recorded on December 13. Temperatures climb to the 70s!

Black comedy movie ***Gremlins***, released on June 8, is set during Christmas time. It's a huge commercial success.

1985

Cabbage Patch Dolls become the most successful dolls in toy history. This year alone, sales of the Cabbage Patch crew grow to more than $600 million.

- **Teddy Ruxpin** charms shoppers; he's an animatronic talking bear that moves his mouth and eyes as he reads stories through a built-in tape deck. Teddy sells out quickly at Christmas.

- Hasbro's **Transformers** are among the top selling toys at Christmas.

- *One Magic Christmas* is the yuletide film of the year.

1986

- The game *Pictionary* is introduced and becomes a favorite pastime this Christmas.
- ABC presents *The Christmas Toy* by The Jim Henson Company. The made-for-TV movie is introduced by **Kermit the Frog**.
- *The Nutcracker*, released on November 26, is a dance film enhanced by costumes and sets designed by Maurice Sendak.

1987

Saturday Night Live stars of this year are pictured in a skit entitled "The Assimilated Jew's Hanukkah."

- *A Garfield Christmas Special* is released on December 21. The animated short is nominated for a Primetime Emmy.

- Hasbro's **Pogo Ball**, an inflatable ball with a platform to stand on, resembles the planet Saturn. Children stand on the platform, squeeze the ball with their feet, and jump and bounce around—they even jump rope!

- **Sylvanian Families** animal figures are on top of children's Christmas lists for three years.

1988

Actor and comedian Pee Wee Herman releases **Christmas in the Playhouse**. On the show he makes a one-and-one-half-mile-long list for Santa. Some consider this the hippest TV Christmas special ever.

- The Care Bears continue to be popular and offer their take on a classic Christmas tale with the animated film **Care Bears: The Nutcracker**.

- The **bread machine** arrives, to home bakers' delight. However, it proves to be not as good as the old-fashioned way of making bread, and many are returned after Christmas.

1989

The **Berlin Wall** is dismantled, starting in November. This historic event culminates with the opening, after 28 years, of the Brandenburg Gate on December 22, in time for Christmas traffic.

- On Christmas Day 1989, **Eastern Europe** is permitted to celebrate Christmas openly after many years, upon the collapse of Communist rule. For the first time in the region's history, masses are broadcast live.

- **Game Boy** is introduced and the portable handheld toy is a sensation at holiday time.

- Promising to preserve Christmas memories for years to come, the **video camera** is a popular yuletide gift.

- *It Nearly Wasn't Christmas*, a movie made for TV, stars Charles Durning as Santa.

Remembering the **1990s**

Jim Henson's irreverent and lovable gang starred in 1992's A Muppet Christmas Carol, *helping kick off the nineties on a happy note. Yuletides this decade were marked by events like the December 1991 release of hostage Terry Anderson and the 1995 launch of online auction site eBay. Block-buster movies included holiday hit* Home Alone. A Nightmare Before Christmas, The Santa Clause, *and* Toy Story *also entertained seasonal audiences. Plush purple Barneys, Beanie Babies, Mighty Morphin Power Rangers, Tickle Me Elmos, and Furbys were among the decade's top Christmas gifts. It was the end of an era with Bob Hope's last USO Christmas tour during Operation Desert Storm, but his warmth and humor remain a gift to treasure.*

1990

- In a year of movie blockbusters, including *Teenage Mutant Ninja Turtles*, *Ghost*, and *Pretty Woman*, the **holiday classic *Home Alone*** launches child star Macaulay Culkin into superstardom and spawns two sequels.

- **Video gamers** have plenty to choose from when compiling holiday wish lists. This is the year of *Final Fantasy, Super Mario World*, and the first 3D platform game, *Alpha Waves*. Woot!

Associated Press Chief Middle East Correspondent **Terry Anderson** is at last released from captivity in Lebanon in December; he was held hostage for more than six years. Anderson is seen here with his sister, who fought diligently for his release.

- As the Soviet Union and its satellite states dissolve during the course of the year, **Mikhail Gorbachev** resigns as president with an historic speech on December 25.

- The popular TV series *Home Improvement*, starring Tim Allen, premieres in September. Its Christmas episodes become legendary in the ensuing eight years the series runs.

- Although online holiday shopping doesn't take off for a few more years, the number of computers using the Internet reaches one million, as the **first Web browser** is introduced by Tim Berners-Lee.

1992

Purple dinosaur Barney, adored by toddlers the world over, is ubiquitous on TV screens and in stores. A plush version is a big hit with the under-five set at holiday time.

- The **Mall of America**, the world's largest shopping mall at this time, opens its doors on August 11. With more than 250 stores, the shopping mecca's sales force swells to about 13,000 during the holiday season.

- The ever-popular Jim Henson Muppet gang appears in the movie *A Muppet Christmas Carol*.

- The **largest Christmas pudding** on record is made in Lancashire, Great Britain, and tips the scale at 7,231 pounds. Come hungry!

Jennings Osborne of Little Rock, Arkansas, mounts one of the **largest residential displays of Christmas lights** in history, with three million lights. After being successfully sued by neighbors, he donates his extravaganza to Walt Disney World.

- Offbeat animated Tim Burton film *The Nightmare Before Christmas* hits it big this year. Is it a Halloween film? A Christmas film? Nobody knows for sure, but it's still a crowd pleaser. Average ticket price? About four dollars.

- The hit TV series *Mighty Morphin Power Rangers* spawns a series of action figures that sell out as soon as they hit store shelves.

- Does the phrase **"Original Nine"** mean anything to you? If it does, you know this is the year the first Beanie Babies are unleashed on an unsuspecting public, creating a craze that would last for years. The Original Nine? Spot the Dog, Squealer the Pig, Patti the Platypus, Cubbie the Bear, Chocolate the Moose, Pinchers the Lobster, Splash the Orca, Legs the Frog, and Flash the Dolphin.

1994

Frank Sinatra delights fans with a compilation album of Christmas classics, many re-mastered from the original "78" recordings. Tracks include "White Christmas," "Jingle Bells," and "Winter Wonderland."

People living in the U.K. and France could, for the first time, travel *underwater* to visit grandmother. The tunnel under the English Channel, popularly known as the **"Chunnel,"** opens in May.

Holiday movie fare includes Disney feature *The Santa Clause*, starring Tim Allen as a reluctant Kris Kringle forced to take the reins of the magic sleigh. The film's popularity spawns two sequels.

Many a stocking is stuffed by Reese's latest and greatest confection, the **Nutrageous** bar, crammed with peanuts, peanut butter, and Hershey's chocolate.

1995

While the **Coca Cola** Company continues its traditional approach to holiday packaging—its "Santa" images are classic— the **Pepsi Cola** Company gives its holiday packaging a cool new twist with holographic treatments.

- Europe enjoys a peaceful Christmas: the **Dayton Agreement**, suspending hostilities in the Yugoslav wars, is signed on December 14 in Paris.

- Christmas in space: six years after its launch, the *Galileo* **spacecraft** arrives at Jupiter.

- Figures **Woody and Buzz Lightyear,** from the popular Disney/Pixar smash *Toy Story,* compete with decidedly low-tech bottle-cap game **Pogs** for dominance of the holiday toy market.

- Just in time for Christmas, the Internet auction site **eBay** is launched. The first item sold: a broken laser pointer, for the princely sum of $14.83.

1996

Sixteen-year-old First Daughter **Chelsea Clinton** has been studying ballet since the age of four; this year, she dances the role of the Favorite Aunt in the Washington, D.C. Ballet's production of *The Nutcracker*.

- During November, the **Dow Jones Industrial Average** grows by leaps and bounds, enriching the coffers of many holiday shoppers.

- No toy approaches the popularity of **"Tickle Me Elmo,"** Tyco's giggling hit. Even though the official retail price is $28.99, Elmo sells out quickly and frantic parents are eager to shell out hundreds of dollars for the hot toy.

1997

Bobs Candy Co. developed a 1950s Keller-created machine that produced the crook in the **candy cane** automatically. By the 1990s, the company becomes the world's largest manufacturer of candy canes, with more than 40 million dollars in sales.

- Fidel Castro had prohibited Christmas celebrations in 1969. In December of this year, he permits the **people of Cuba** to celebrate the holiday once again.

- On December 25, **movie box office** receipts pass six million dollars. *Titanic*, *The Postman*, and *Mr. Magoo* are some of the year's big hits.

1998

The **world's largest gingerbread man**, 11 feet tall, is made by high school students in The Woodlands, Texas. An official from *The Guinness Book of World Records* confirms his measurements.

- *Rudolph the Red-Nosed Reindeer*, an animated film based on the Christmas song, is released. The cast includes John Goodman, Whoopi Goldberg, Debbie Reynolds, and Bob Newhart.

- Electronic toy **Furby** is a must-have gift this holiday season. In 1998 alone, 1.8 million Furby robots are sold. The speaking capabilities of these toys are translated into 24 languages.

- On December 1, in Leipzig, Germany, the largest detached **Advent calendar** is exhibited; it measures 857.21 square meters.

- On Christmas Eve, 29 Canadian and six German veterans who'd battled each other at Ortona in 1943 come together for a **reconciliation Christmas Eve** Mass and dinner at Santa Marie di Costantinopoli church.

1999

- Animated video *Mickey's Once Upon a Christmas* is released on December 7. Kelsey Grammer is the narrator.

- Based on the 1999 population count of Europe and North America, Santa Claus must visit 42,466,666 homes within a 12-hour period on Christmas Eve—that's **983 trips down the chimney per second!**

- **One in three men wait until Christmas Eve** to finish their shopping. What popular last-minute Christmas gift might they and others get for family and friends? *A Century of Christmas Memories*—a book to be cherished for the next century to come!

Merry Christmas!

The **world's largest snowman**, according to *The Guinness Book of World Records*, is built in Bethel, Maine. This frozen fellow stands 113 feet, seven inches tall.

Picture Credits